The Way Out

The Way Out

🌿 poems by
Lisa Sewell

Alice James Books
Farmington, Maine

Library of Congress Cataloging-in-Publication Data
Sewell, Lisa, 1960-
        The way out: poems / by Lisa Sewell—1st ed.
        p. cm.
        ISBN 1-882295-17-X
        I. Title
PS3569.E8853W38   1998
811'.54—dc21   97-4136
                                    CIP

Printed in the United States of America
First Edition
9 8 7 6 5 4 3 2 1

Book design:	Julia Sewell
Cover photograph:	Francesca Woodman, from *Angel Series* courtesy of George and Betty Woodman
Author photograph:	Leslie Seligman

Alice James Books gratefully acknowledges support
from the University of Maine at Farmington and
the National Endowment for the Arts.

Alice James Books are published by the
Alice James Poetry Cooperative, Inc.,
an affiliate of the University of Maine at Farmington.
Alice James Books
98 Main Street
Farmington, Maine 04938

For my parents, George and Edith
and for my sister Julia

In memory of
Ori Scharf
Lloyd Ehrenberg

Acknowledgments

Acknowledgment is made to the editors of the following journals in which some of these poems, or earlier versions of them, have appeared:

The Greensboro Review: "Refuge" and "Ornithology." *Hootenanny:* "A Dedication" and "Telling Them Apart." *The Indiana Review:* "The Swimmer." *The Massachusetts Review:* "Inheritance." *Michigan Quarterly Review:* "The Miraculous." *Passages North:* "The Empty Dish," "Health," "One of the Foolish Women," "The Announcement," "Expulsion" (as "Then I Read About Eve in *Paradise Lost*"), "Surrender," "Two Lessons in the Sacred," and "The Denied." *Pequod:* "More or Less," and "Evolution." *Southern Poetry Review:* "Expulsion" (as "Then I Read About Eve in *Paradise Lost*"). *Zone 3:* "At the Heart of the Season." *third coast:* "Human Nature."

I am grateful to the Fine Arts Work Center at Provincetown, Blue Mountain Center, the Virginia Center for the Creative Arts and the Corporation of Yaddo for residencies during which many of these poems were written, and to the Massachusetts Cultural Council and the Somerville Arts Council for support which was crucial to the completion of this manuscript.

Contents

Four

. . . whom can we ever turn to
in our need? Not angels, not humans,
and already the knowing animals are aware
that we are not really at home in
our interpreted world.

Rainer Maria Rilke

One

✹ Chorale

Clearly I'm the volitional subject and though not violent
I am haunted. The lost, the never felt and unhinged voices
sing through me these insomniac nights of my own exile,

not theirs, like streams that bank the rocks
and dirt slopes of disappointment. I thought each day,
and every continuous week free, meant *precious,*

worth guarding. I've imagined their sleep, weight
on mattresses in rooms that don't exist and who would protect,
who aid and abet them—but never the texture of their hair

or skin, eye color, limb. Their songs, like chalk
along asphalt, mark the boundaries of inclusion, the games
I won't play, redrawing the line I stepped over one morning

one July. Blame the selfish gene, the animal planet
I was born to, the twist in my nature that stilled
each voice, and kept them in check, coveted, leashed,

a muffled chorus that accompanies me
along these bland vistas. Imagine, if I had freed
just one and let it carry across the water or alight

among the hawthorn's strict branches. Imagine gestation
and then I'm someone's mother, loved, hated or ignored.
If I have been mistaken, giving up life and more life

to safeguard mine, this humming din,
this ghost song of my own and another's making
must be the all that I have left.

❧ Trompe L'oeil

It's like the slap
you know is coming that still shocks
as it completes you: his mouth
with its serious expression, that familiar
line, *you deserve better.* The puzzle's ready
to be dismantled and no matter how long
I stand before the mirror
I can't locate what he's noticed
when he makes his decision. It's why
I try to keep things
penultimate, as if by force of will
I'll stave off famine or by sleight
of hand, a trick of the eye, the glamorous
Paris showgirl can be made to cancel out
the old hag who seems to dominate
once you notice her. I try to recognize
the signs, try not to hex it
by thinking this is the last time
his hand will graze my sex, last taste
of his sweat, last pulse of him
emptying inside. Transfixed
by his arching up to meet my *yes,* I don't notice
the mob gathered at the horizon, waving bottles
picking up sticks and momentum
or pay attention to my own
anxious scent of premonition, so I'm stunned
when I stop squinting and see in his face
the darkling flock of birds
descending, not the gulls
I had put there, who in their forward motion
seem to lift up and fly.

❧ Surrender

As it glides along the ciliated tube,
the fertilized egg divides
innumerable times, floats a bit
then burrows into the rich wall of the uterus.
It's crucial, that time of digging-in,
to the blastula's survival,
to the gills and the delicate fishtail
and the blind fish eyes. It would love
the salted heartbeat without question
if it could love—
but it only wants the process
that's been triggered to continue.
Amphibian, quiescent, it knows nothing
of parking lots, speed, or desire
or that sometimes I pull him inside
just to feel my own weight
crushed against the sheets.
Conception is no miracle,
no burst of light that flashes
love, love. It's a pin-prick
and the frantic division of chromosomes
that sets things in motion.
What makes it so hard
to give in, and let the momentum
take me? What makes it so clear
that I must stop it? I watch others grow large
with that leap of faith,
though it may be a mistake
and they may suffer intolerably.
Such faith courses and burns
beneath my skin also, but something else
in me refuses. What am I
that each time my body has signaled its power
I relinquish it without question
to common sense and the machinery?

❧ The Good Servant

*And the Lord said unto Satan, Hast thou considered
my servant Job, that there is none like him in the earth.* Job 1:8

I have never understood the lesson about the man
who remained faithful despite punishment without measure

or reason, who loved the thought of heaven more
than reliable earth and flesh, but when my love spoke

of the life unfolding inside me as a neutral bunch of cells, a tumor
he would have no part of, and assured me of nothing,

not even the next day, I began to understand something
about that man and about his God, also.

I thought that when Satan came with his report and proposal,
perhaps God recognized some vestigial gesture, a turn of phrase

that recalled the archangel he had fashioned and lost,
and was filled with an awful longing, a fear that registered

in the enormity of destruction unleashed on that single,
ordinary man in the absence of any sign of hope

or care. In the end, the story teaches the rewards of fealty,
that suffering can illustrate faith, but because my own love

has been tested and endures through each
improbable day, what I believe is that Job continued to love

in spite of himself and all that he knew, that most likely
he couldn't do anything but persist,

for his love moved inside him as relentlessly
as the blood that traveled his veins and arteries.

Later, he did his best not to censure or blame,
and to accept God's need to repay his suffering, the excessive

grateful display as he blessed, one thousand fold, this man
whose love could not be unmade, a man who had seen

into the white empty space at the heart of the whirlwind
and did not turn away.

🍂 Health

Only when I starved myself could I appease the god
who named me. I was almost pure—like the hawk
who is all appetite and speed. Every rib rose up
beneath my skin, utterly legible, proof
that I was not like the others: governed, subject to urges.

Anyone who looked at me could see I had taken matters
into my own hands. This new body, with its insulating layers
of tissue distorts all my efforts: my gait
betrays misgivings, my false step. Each morning
I labor to build myself from desperation and thin air,
and to make the blank faces light up, *Yes, yes. Exactly.*

A pocket of space swallows my words and spits them out
slightly altered. Most of the time
I don't know what I've said and then I try
to correct it. If I could return to the moment
when the bones hollowed to reveal their true
formation, I would be myself again.

But like the mockingbird, when I reach
for the one note that will perfectly unfold my nature
I find myself in the middle of some melody
I've heard somewhere, and then another and another.

🍂 Dream of Winter

Even though it's Spring when I return to her
and the natural light is generous
to everything it illuminates, I get cranky.
I lose track of myself. She thinks time stops
while I'm away, that I am like the birches
who fold into themselves to suffer the cold
but underneath the earth I grow more different
every day and there are marks on me she
wouldn't recognize. What she told Jove
wasn't entirely true. I wanted to get away
from the warmth, her year-round August.
That unfamiliar field looked like liberty
to my eyes and when the earth cracked open
I was dazzled, excited, and I even liked
that he was rough when he grabbed me.
He's strange at times, childish, but not so awful
as she's made him out. I've come to love the damp
muddy air, the tawdry candlelight, his teeth
at my neck, my ear. She says
how can you live there, the soot, the closeness,
after all I did to raise you in sunshine
how can you stand it? I tell you it isn't paradise
I've been banished from, but the illusion
of safety, that I roamed her empire
free of despair. From here I can see
that she was desperate then too,
overpopulating the earth
in her excessive joy—was it really any better
than her cold grief later? If only
I could confide in her again, tell of his betrayals
and roving eye, the botched pregnancies.
With a chill in the air, I could bear

to let her hold me, and bear to feel
how much she needs that—goddess of fruitfulness
who I once believed could keep me from harm,
and whose love I imagined
to be unconditional.

🖉 Circe, After his Departure

Through it has been months, and she only knew him
for a brief, heady time, she still thinks of him,
still gazes idly out at a horizon on which no vague blur
or bright spot that might grow into a ship or bird appears,
and that from the vantage point
of middle life looks curved but limited.
He is like desire, or the marker
for desire that eludes her grasp in order to keep itself
perpetually in motion. But it's much more specific
than that. There's the way he held her jaw
in both his hands when he kissed her, the animal yearning
that crossed his face when she asked him to.
She would like to forget about him
for she knows her love is the door to loss
and to the joy that accompanies, precedes
or follows. Aren't they the same—misery
and pleasure—one being the underside that makes the other
possible and makes it intolerable to live
without each? She would open him up and crawl back
into that spot below his heart that marks her absence
if it would teach him the possibility
of union, and the necessity of such promise and belief.
If she had the chance she would tell him
it's like the moment before you come,
when you feel impossibly grateful, that moment
before the moment you return from nowhere
having lost yourself, however briefly,
and are soaked through with disappointment
and with the knowledge that we are hopelessly enclosed
by the measure of our skins, and the wetness that shone
as he slipped out of her, the glistening
trail he left on her thigh were only residue,
but are nevertheless, the very meat
and sustenance required to survive.

🌾 The Darkened Room

After the heart had healed somewhat and steadied
in its cage, after sleep returned, visiting past dawn and well

into morning, there wasn't much to talk about
when he called. Some marriages

are based in common things: books, habits,
where you come from. With others,

it's as if love were the soul, and when the two
previously separate selves join they form the body.

I don't believe in the soul, but I'm afraid
and what I think about now is the way

we'd lie together on his bed for a long time
without speaking. As I went about my business,

leaving the house to teach or study
or have coffee with friends, in my mind I was still

in the darkened room, breathing. It's wrong to suffer
fools, throw good money or love what annuls you

like it's a house on fire that you don't leave,
despite the smoke, the walls collapsing.

In my dream, I was kneeling
in the charred carapace, sifting through debris

as if I would never turn away
the apparition that arrives disguised as fulfillment,

and the ash that darkened my fingers,
the crest of one temple, my hair and lips,

could mark me in recognition of who I had been
and preparation for how I would live.

The Way Out of the Hospital

When the constriction that spent winter
residing in my chest finally tightened its grip,
I drove to the emergency room and turned myself over
to the doctor and nurses, to Epinephrine
and Theodur, the insinuating drip of the I.V.
But the hospital has been a terrible
disappointment, offering porcelain exposure
instead of stupor and anonymity. You see,
oxygen is too important and asthmatics
are not permitted to sleep and I
have never felt more acutely myself,
propped up on this moveable bed
for observation. At the Museum of Science
the Transparent Woman had blue veins
and red arteries, a brown intestine coiled
in her abdomen. I felt sorry for her: a giantess
who turned the inside into a spectacle. Worst of all,
her heart seemed out of proportion
to reality. Her voice calmly explained
the functioning of the valves and chambers
but no one listened because the heart
was so astonishing as it flickered and glowed.
For three days, the liquid medicine
has made the vein on my wrist
throb with cold, while my own
iridescent heart sounds its faithfulness
on the video screen. Now I am the only one
who has to make an effort, but soon
I'll move about the room unencumbered, breathe
secretly, in silence. For I have paid attention
as air rattled on its journey
through my lungs' smallest pockets and like

the Transparent Woman, I will speak
of the flesh, the blood, sweet oxygen, remembering
this ordinary room, the mild sedative
that finally let me sleep and my own steady breathing
when they told me I could leave.

❧ The Quickening

The night the first real blizzard of the season began,
I remember telling myself *when this is over*
you will feel differently, as if winter
were a garment to wrap around the self, or could preserve me
the way it does the warm-blooded animals,
letting them more than slumber
through the bleakest winter months, their hearts wound down
to a dull tolerable rhythm, their lungs
automatically forcing oxygen through the capillaries—
and all this activity requiring
neither will nor conviction. But Spring came
and to say I felt differently would be inaccurate
or even a lie. When the yellow palm of the sun opened
to reveal the dust motes in the corners and I
pushed the hood back from my eyes, and peeled off layers
of clothing and soot, didn't the same pain
hurry through me? Didn't the quickening of blood
undo time's work, no matter how insistently
I counted off the months? From my window
I can smell the morning and watch
the garish waves of forsythia, the brief
flowering of trees, but what I feel
is nothing like jubilation or relief. Is it possible
to practice contentment, study bliss
or sit at this table and love
the way I fill a chair, hum quietly
through each solitary day, or love the song
my pencil scratches out as it moves across the page.

🌿 **Two**

🍃 The Art of Survival

It's what I love about the half-naked woman
who rises from the sea in the postcard
I keep taped above my bathroom mirror.
"Now that is a woman" I remind myself every morning,

because even with the anchor tied around her neck
it doesn't seem bad to emerge as she does: crowned,
a flounder slung across her shoulders and a cock
in her pants. The worst has happened and the fish

is not about to speak or grant her wishes,
if she has them. She doesn't make it look easy but possible
and despite all that gold leaf around her shining,
it is this world she has chosen.

after a painting by Tabitha Vevers

❦ Inheritance

Every night my father climbed
my mother's body while I lay restless
as the air around their bed and listened
for my name to sound
through the bedroom floor.
I wanted to be made again
from that uneven dark, to reside
for a time in strangeness
or be given a second chance
at the genes for resilience
and the capacity for joy. But she was through
with the hot flashes, the day-long
freeway rides, the body's mess.
My father was a god who stole
my mother from her mother.
He named himself salvation and pushed her
to the knees she crawled back up to earth on.
Now he touches me and seems
to weigh my flesh. He is afraid
of my spreading hips, my menstrual breath.
In his wallet is a picture of me
at nineteen: I am tan and toned
and have the kind of thighs
he'd like to slide between.
Beneath my clinging shorts
and T-shirt I can see the slight paunch:
my mother's belly, her secret dell
with its black trail of mannish hair
descending.

❧ The Thief

Take the way Demeter climbed down
beneath her fields and knelt
before the undergods as a supplicant—
who really knows what particular urge
sent her down there. My mother, too,
valued sacrifice and only left us once
to go god knows where—but she came back
unharmed and apparently untransformed
and that's how I insist on seeing her today:
irresistible with the promise of rescue, always ready
to intervene on my behalf. But every mother has a secret
or a dark god she kneels down to.
What if yours were exactly who you thought
only sadder, and her lies, her deft deceptions
shielded a truth as commonplace
as shoplifting? It's too late to stop her
from spending my adolescence hunched
over a toilet, but sometimes I wish
she hadn't returned to us that day and had remained
in the mysterious world that beckoned.
Is this exile? Is this how Persephone felt
sorting through photographs
from her unremarkable childhood, suddenly aware
that even before she had wandered or bent
to pluck the dark flower, she was lost, that Demeter
never could have saved her?

Empty Dish

Some days Jay's cat—who perhaps
misses Jay or misses his shape
and the shadows he made—comes to her blue
flowered dish and does not cry out
to be fed, but sits and through half-slit eyes
observes the licked cleanness.
She isn't hungry. This is where need
gets met, and she has circled the house
to refind this spot with its promise
of something like satisfaction; just as I,
driven by some other need, return
to the white bowl of the toilet and kneel
when I have nothing to offer, my body empty
as the dish, seeking not to bring up
the acid surge of release, but to feel
the cool enamel, the linoleum against my knees
in a familiar crouch that once seemed
a kind of answer, a way to pray.
If I were a painter, all my women
would face front, lips wide, to show
how the open mouth dwarfs
the other features, as it mimics
what disappears or cancels in mathematics:
the multiplicative identity, the zero.

❦ My Body in Japan

1.

In Tokyo, my fantasy is to eat
at an Isakaiya in Kabukucho or my own
neighborhood, one I can return to
night after night, and sit on the tatami
with my legs folded, not underneath me
like chicken wings, but crossed in front,
thighs open: I order beer and a basket
of those small salted shrimp you can pop
into your mouth like peanuts, and read
one of the pornographic comic books
they keep at the magazine rack,
and no one watches me and no one asks
if I am married.

2.

The closest I ever came to being famous
was when I bleached my hair blonde
and cropped it to an inch
around my head. On the trains everyone
stared openly, my students screamed
when I walked into the classroom.
I had already been eating on the subway,
and smoking in public despite my friend
Etsuko's warning. On weekends, each new man
was a layer of skin to shield me
from the one who knew me best.
I needed new teeth at my breast,
a different melody to hum with.
I took each cock between my lips
to make my tongue forget a particular
acrid taste, a lost brother,
that other perfect shape.

3.
When the doctor returned to the waiting room
her English was precise and brief. *Congratulations*
she smiled, holding out the slide
with its milky urine stain.

She took a thimbleful of blood, then deftly
fingered my cervix. Everything seemed
to be in order. I was on the table. My body
was a bed, a furnace, a liquid nest.

Inserting something else between my legs, she flipped
a switch. On the screen I saw the universe
with its smear of stars and milky way, bright planets
looped into their orbits. The germinal pulse

was a silent bleat, and as the minute
white arrow zeroed in the doctor said *See it,*
that's the fetus, and here, the arrow moved, *is the ovary,*
the broken follicle.

4.
In Nikko water bubbles up from the earth, warm
with mineral secrets. Steam rises. A light snow
chills my shoulders.

My students say you must enter the pools
three times to become beautiful and I do
as I'm instructed. Among the careful rocks

and stunted trees, my legs grow heavy
as a man's legs, but each time I emerge,
something loosens its grip and my womb
gives off its hidden lantern light.

5.

I need to talk about later and my body on that table for an hour with the glucose drip in my arm and my legs in stirrups until my muscles ached. No one told me anything. I didn't take my legs out of those metal rings and rest my thighs. I didn't know the waiting was a mistake. The doctor came with her blade, with her assistants, with Valium that made my head expand and fill with air but just before it burst there was cold wet and terrific pain. I thought if I screamed she would stop a moment, the way my dentist would stop drilling if I lifted my right hand from the arm-rest. But she kept scraping and swabbing and I kept screaming even though she told me to keep quiet. *Shut your mouth* she hissed and I remembered how in some Japanese films the women gave birth with just a few low grunts and a light sweat on their foreheads. When I looked for the doctor's eyes behind her glasses and mask I saw myself reflected back, foreign-one, gaijin, outsider.

❧ More or Less

What do you do when your friend says
he doesn't know how much longer
he can do this—and *this* is everything:
speaking, breathing, swallowing too
because apple juice, iced coffee—
anything thicker than water—makes him choke.
What I did was watch for half an hour
as he coughed and cried, keeping my eyes on him
until he collapsed. And I don't know
if this is right or good, but I wanted him to see
that I could look and look as if my watching
were the one thing I had left to offer
as a friend, and could restore
some portion of what this disease has taken.
I wanted to make his unmaking palatable, something
I could bear. Three years ago
if you had asked what he is like,
I'd have said *thin, blue-eyed, more or less
like you.* I sat on Lloyd's red brick patio
beside the dense camellia bushes and the pale
bougainvillea, wishing
I could visit every week, and rest there with him,
in companionable silence. But it had been a year
since my last visit and the difficult
important words—*comfortable, readjustment,
window, rest*—had to be repeated
and even then I drove away with many
unanswered questions, remembering Julia
at the hospital on Roosevelt Island
who could only communicate
by moving her eyes upward for *yes.*
When I apologized
for not writing and said

I think about him often, Lloyd said
he thinks about me too
and I consider that a blessing. Even now
I think his love must be hovering
at my shoulder, like those celluloid angels
who keep watch over Berlin—silent, full
of forgiveness, and listening.

🌿 Refuge

Driving down the coast
toward the last time I would see him,
I had worried, not feeling up
to watching as he gagged and cried
or to eating my own lunch
while his caregiver filled a large syringe
with green pea soup and injected it
into the plastic tube
attached to his stomach, but you never know
where sanctuary lies, and forget the way
it can arrive like sleep
after long hours of insomnia, or like everything
you ever dreamed of—
In the weeks since that visit
it has begun to seem that I went willingly
into hell and climbed on Satan's
terrible thighs toward the mixed
purgatorial light, the refuge
of Lloyd's blurred and failing gaze.
After that I expected him
to be there, a different Lloyd
from the one I had known ten years, but one
I would count on. How good it is
to have that day like the dried petals
of a dogwood flower pressed into a book—
startling for their intricate transparency
and the penetrating scent of musk and decay.
The last time, more than anything,
I wanted to touch him, to cover
his flat muscleless hand with my own
while he slept, or run my palm across or kiss
the smooth plate of his forehead which glistened

with the effort of his life, and beneath which
lay his brain, shrouded, almost unreachable,
but still firing off its singular
electric impulses, steadily ticking
through the last hours
I would spend in his grace.

❦ A Dedication

When they opened him up, the doctors
must have been impressed
by the state of his liver:
that much damage in only 27 years
suggests a single-mindedness almost like courage.
I wish I could see it that way,
but I miss him and after five years
I still think about his body—how for four days
it lay alone, and his father,
the one chosen to enter the silent apartment,
had to face it alone also, and held upright
by his two uncertain narrow legs, he looked down
on his son. I hope all the blood vessels
beneath the skin were still intact,
that his eyes were shut and that he looked
not like just any dead abandoned body
but like him, like Ori.
It was probably the first time in years
his father had seen him naked: the white belly
protruding above the dense mat
and sturdy cock, and the sparse
red hairs that ringed his nipples.
Did he bend down, and without thinking, touch
the dense skin that had once flushed pink
with promise or smooth the hair
from his forehead? And was it then
that his father's legs collapsed?
Think of seeing that you have been undone
by a dream of your own making, a hand
composed of cells and tissues
that still hold a map
to your own chromosomes. Two policemen

had to carry Ori's father out
between them. A tall man
with hair already prematurely white,
he couldn't have crawled away
from that basement apartment with its stained rug
and yellowed shades, its triumphant ghost.

❧ The Denied

Often I return to that room—abject,
mortified—where after weeks of quiet,
an occasional moan or singing, something fell
hard and I opened the door to find my grandmother
collapsed. All the shades were drawn and the air
had that hospital scent of medicine
and stale urine. When I tried to move her back
onto the bed, I felt her thick
frightened weight, our shared weariness
and panic but mostly fury at my parents
who had left for the day. I can't forget
how I wished I hadn't heard, how I knew even then
if I had passed her in a diner, her hair in a net,
the left lens of her glasses shattered, with her sweet roll
and black coffee and Parliament cigarettes, muttering
in Yiddish and trying to catch my eye, I would have denied
that I knew her. For years I have offered up this scene
as the touchstone of my nature, evidence
that I lack the portion of chromosome
that carries the genes for courage, human decency.
But recently, I have begun to practice
another kind of compassion and have looked back,
full of tenderness, for the girl I was, especially
for the moments when we lay on the damp
grainy floor exhausted, and with my arms
still wrapped around her impossible, mortal shape,
both of us rested, the only sound our labored breathing
and my weeping, as we waited
with a faith I have not felt again, for me
to find the strength to lift her.

❧ Two Lessons in the Sacred

1.

My mother only cares for what she can taste
and smell, for her the life of the body
is all we have—she wants hers fired to ash
and scattered. What would she think of August
in Madagascar, when families
who have received messages
bring the dead out of their graves, wrap the bones
in new shrouds and briefly dance with them?
There is something beautiful
about going up in fire—the heat, the immense
consuming whoosh of oxygen—but it seems
too clean, too absolute. Like my mother,
I put my faith in the physical world,
but in death doesn't the body continue
on its path, and isn't that unmaking
worth enduring? If death steals
my mother's essence, won't I continue to want
whatever is left? Before speech, before
understanding, I knew her cool lips
against my forehead, the scent
of her hair and breath. Of course I've also hated
her body as thoroughly as my own, but I'd like to think
that I could overcome my revulsion
and the smell, care for my mother's body
even in the stages of decay—
that I'd tenderly oil her powdery bones,
cover her again in a newly woven cloth. Perhaps
before I laid her back onto her bed
I would waltz with her in slow expansive circles,
keeping time under my breath and humming the tunes
I remember, making the room spin.

2.

When I ride my first bus
across the rice-green Bengal plain
and see the unbending line of the horizon,
and the pale sheet that stretches to illuminate
the gleaming backs of buffalo, the bending
and slow moving bodies, the goats
and yak, I feel my bags and tired body
fill with light and start to rise.
Beneath this sky it seems a simple thing
to turn away from the material, to lock your door
one morning and leave with an umbrella and orange robe.
But the body persists. It is the only thing
we are given. In Benares, holiest
of holies, final stop on the pilgrimage for the dead,
wallahs can be hired to oversee the day long cremation.
The poorer families must tend their own pyres,
keeping watch until the skull explodes.
There is nothing to take away from that place
except the burning that stays in your clothes
and the long memory of the journey.

Three

🖋 One of the Foolish Women

So the Lord blessed the latter end of
Job more than the beginning. Job 42:12

But it's difficult for her to feel that way,
even with the fourteen thousand sheep, the thousand
yoke of oxen. *For my sighing cometh*
before I eat, and my roarings are poured out
like the waters. She cannot bring herself to love
the impostor children who never dwelt
in her body, and belong to God as well.

After the seventh day of silence, while he
and his three friends spun out their endless arguments,
she walked across the field, the ten shrouds
weightless in her arms, to the fallen house
and her children's bodies. *The Lord gave,*
the Lord hath taken away.

She wants to talk about the ashes, the oxen slain,
the sheep in flames and their son's house
collapsing, but he refuses. What she remembers
is the dry air, the wind and the messenger,
And I only am escaped alone to tell thee.

He is a good servant. He believes in his rewards
and dotes on the new daughters as if their beauty
reflects his triumph, as if he has already forgotten
the names of the others.

When she cries at night, he covers his ears.
He has tried to tell her what he has learned:
truthfulness, faith, humility, fear, but she speaks
as one of the foolish women speaks
and will not be taught.

❧ Forty Years

I know my father loved my mother
when they married. He gave up forty years
of free-wheeling and drove his MG all the way
to California: Camarillo, Pt. Mugu,
San Vicente. I think she blossomed
in that dry clear light and my father
made her beautiful—it's in every shot
from their first summers in Echo Park:
the camera's eye on her, ripe
with adoration. And from the way my mother
gazes back, young, aware
of the ache in him her body arouses, I know
he cherished her, no matter what
she claims today. So when a new man approaches
in his unfamiliar body, and everything
requires interpretation, the beseeching look, the smile
he holds out to me, I make a prayer
of their early love and their willingness, so dense
and headstrong. Forty years.
I can hardly bear to think of them today, yoked
in unyielding reciprocal silence.
The other night, I read aloud for my friend's
two-year-old son, and with his sturdy body
pressed against my chest, I knew
there is no milder heaviness, no sweeter
burden. I have been that weight.
I lent sweetness to my mother's life
and lived in the glint of my father's eye.
How I have wanted to remain a stay
against the bitterness that washes their days
or to be the vessel in which the seeds
of their earliest devotion find shelter and radiate.

🌿 Numerology

If two marks duplicity, the separation
that can only lead to doubt, then why provide the garden

with its intoxicating green, the perfumed mouths of flowers
gaping open? Why let them believe
that they were made for one another?

I like to imagine them there together without the third,
intrusive voice, without instruction, and Adam's pleasure
when she turned her face towards him and opened her eyes

to match his look, his hunger. Afterwards, she rehearsed
the scene to locate the moment when everything
shifted, and later still, tried to recall the smell of his skin,

the precise hue of the leaves and sky
as he moved above her. That he volunteered
and went with her into Canaan, does not reassure me:

the sounds that passed between them no longer meant
the same things, beside each word or syllable a gap opened.
If he had said "no one will ever love you,"

it would have been less cruel. If I know anything, I know
the hesitation in his touch, the reluctance that came later.

❧ Telling Them Apart

The girl is the one who does not recognize
her own face in the glass until too late,
until long after the voice—call it God,
call it Freud—has pointed to that other shape (*less fair,*
less winning soft) and instructed her desire.

She thinks her eyes have always flinched away
or paused, bewildered, disappointed, when the mirror
finds her and cannot recall lingering there
dumb with love. When they walk together

along the street, he presents his firm profile
to remind her: *He for God only, she*
for God in him, his eyes fixed on what is ahead—
a crowded sidewalk, a movie screen, the future.

Of course he loves her. She's the most talented girl yet
to wrap her mouth around his cock, and he can teach her
things: the names of the animals. But she is the one
who walks awry, her whole body dipping towards him,

irresistibly drawn to the flesh and bones
of her making, as if she wants to be turned back
into a rib, allowed to rise and fall beside the others
and rest just below his heart, forever.

Expulsion

Then I finally understood that the angel
when it comes will not be mild, but horrible
like Raphael who came down to paradise
with his warning and had six wings, not two—
one pair that covered his face, and one that wrapped
around his feet while a third flapped the air
behind his shoulders.

He must have seemed more gargoyle than cherub
with unnatural appetites and words that undid her, a beauty
that promised certainty not comfort. And after feeding an angel,
how could Adam—mere clay, God's handyman—appease her?
Their shared history, the familiar gestures
and syllables of his love-making would seem
a kind of suffocation beneath the roar
of those wings and even his explanation of her dream
must appear limited.

When the serpent opened his mouth, Eve might have seen
that pink flickering tongue and known enough.
Instead she closed the door on day
after day of the same. The second angel
came to lead them out of paradise and Eve
was ready. Holding up her binoculars
to drink in the terror of his slow approach, she smiled
despite her fear and regret, and felt
somewhat like a god herself to have called
such a thing forward, those wings coming toward her.

🌿 Choke Cherries

When I crush one between my thumb
and forefinger, it leaves a bad smell
on my hands. Old or new they look like poison,

but I'd like to eat one just to see. It isn't death
I'm after but the journey deep into winter,
the epiphany, the stupor.

The beautiful ice-man returns
my glance and smiles his ice smile
before he walks away, and though the carriage
of his shoulders warns not to follow,
I do, I go anyway.

❧ Love Poem

Certainly I have exhausted myself with patience.
I don't turn men to stone
but they get a little cruel, a little colder
and it may be that passion changes me—
though in an animal we appreciate
the unguarded display, in a woman
it's another thing entirely. Think of Medusa.
How she must have balked
when the only man brave enough to approach
kept his eyes averted. I think I'm just a tall girl
with desires like any other, trying to see
what I look like before my features
compose themselves into the face I imagine
others must love, as if the answer
were any clearer than the question. At the exhibit
of medical experiments, in one photo, a woman
whose breasts have been painfully disfigured smiles
for the camera, perhaps as she had for her lover,
her eyes dark with what seems
like pleasure, her head tilted at the angle of desire,
and even as I recoiled, wondering
what was she thinking, she made me love her—
as I loved the lonely German Shepherd
who broke his chain one evening to accompany me
on my walk. His gait was slightly off center
and he seemed full of wants
at the height of summer but I didn't mind
when he brushed against my legs.
Was it faith or foolishness that filled his heart
as he galloped through the heavy air to meet me?

❧ The Passion of the Queen

It's a familiar story: reckless ardor
and brokenness, and Dido lunatic
with disappointment. She must have noticed
the restlessness in his eyes and loved him more
for it, but what if she hadn't chosen the pyre
and had found the patience to recover,
as from a stroke, practicing first
the simple tasks like sleeping and eating,
then moving on to the more complex
responsibilities? Maybe her desolation
would have exhausted itself and dulled
to a steady ache, the sharp occasional throb—
and then one morning, say a man took shape
at the edge of her vision, and lingered there
until something inside her knelt down
and wept. Even if this new one
had disappointed, turned scared as well, wouldn't she
have welcomed the rush? Imagine her gratitude
when that dusky fire reignited, proving
that the broken heart can still build
within—can pump oxygen-rich blood to the dry
dormant places, staining the delicate skin
of the chest and neck, releasing
its blossom of flames.

🌿 Messenger

Two nights before the wedding
my first love comes back, and this time too
I get down on my knees and bang palms
and wrists against plaster walls
to illustrate my devastation. He is the one
who taught me that a man could love
as fiercely as a mother, that I could come
three times but in my dream
he is not generous, and my need
to hear him say it—*someone
else, someone new*—the true
condemning sentence, is so acute
I smash a jar of vinegar
against the wall above his head
and scare myself, though my violence
is not extreme or unusual. I know the heart
is a misguided book and memory
as convoluted as the gray matter
that contains us, but why should bad news
need repeating and so many years late?
In a dream, can you misapprehend
the messenger's intentions,
set the elliptical narrative down
the wrong path? What if he came
not to prove again that I
could be discarded
but to bless?

❧ The Announcement

When the angel comes into her room
and points with his long finger
her hand opens and the cloth and needle
clatter to the floor. She has already finished
the most difficult stitching,
the lily's delicate stem,
and is startled out of lethargy by desire—
not for the Word or the child
who will drive her out of her life into a night
with stars that move away or shine
differently each time she raises her eyes.
No, she sees that he is naked underneath his robes,
that his chest rises when he breathes or speaks.
There is nothing soft in him, and she wants that
too, and to see the ceiling bloom
with the shadow of her own limbs
magnified, in motion.
For weeks at night she has lain on her side
and run her hand from shoulder blade to hip.
Some song, some dove's coo has tickled her throat
or was it her ear? She knew then
she had a body but here, late, like a vision
against the bare plaster, is a reason.
She watches his mouth move but hardly hears
the terrible revelation. *Ave.* She whispers, *Gabriel,
make me your Jacob, name me, wrestle me, until morning.*

Four

❧ The Miraculous

Is it really so surprising that at thirty-four
you see life as a stockpile of loss, or that you long
for a fence to ring your yard, the skirts
your mother discarded, domestic ordinariness?

And isn't it almost a given that your hand reaches
towards the heads of small children whose hair
seems to emit a dazzling, irresistible light, that your heart
contracts a little more each time

a friend calls to tell her good news.
The future is no longer the place your real life
will start. These are the dark woods, the middle
of your life, and your guide's instructions

have been spoken to someone else or perhaps to you,
but you couldn't hear. Even so, isn't it time to be grateful
for what the world gives back—the glutinous dough
you punch and slap down that rises again, the tulips

on the mantle that reveal more of their yellow hearts each day
until they collapse—and to marvel that his sweet cock
still responds in your hand, its single eye glistening, eager
to push inside you despite all the ghosts that dream there,

your history of mouths. Isn't it the miraculous,
and not a sorrowful tale that delivers you to this bed,
where his body arches up from all its remorse, regret
and mistakenness, until, joined at the pelvis

and leaning back to see into the other's face, together
you resemble nothing if not wings—
where you might recline as if finally at home
and with his head against your heaving chest, his skull

almost visible beneath his hair and musky scalp,
you lie back and breathe in.

🍂 Human Nature

When someone presses his mouth to mine, I don't hesitate,
I open my lips. But doesn't this willingness
to give myself over look as much like sacrifice
as anything, and only Jesus,
with his heart the size of God's fist, could manage that
and not be plagued. I might ask
those summering geese, white
to the very tips of their feathers, who rise up
and don't care about the pleasure they give—that's not a gift
but their nature, like Nietzsche's birds of prey
who love lambs with their appetites. What if my nature
is to love indiscriminately and with reckless
prodigal haste? What if wired into me, part of the helical
strands of code that made my hair brown and my elbows
bony, is the kiss? When the wheels of their migratory clocks
shift gears, the geese will deafen the air but I'll remain
without instinct or sense, burying my face
in a stranger's neck, as if the sole condition
for my love is that it be accepted and I crave
the jangled heart beating itself
into a frenzy and something tangible
to focus on: the insistent tongue, the hard as nails teeth
which lie just beyond the lips and are as white
as the geese and almost as startling.
The hardest task is to endure. Think of Peter:
when the cock crowed and Jesus looked at him with compassion
and no reproach, he ran. But what I need
is a story that springs from a purely human nature
and teaches good and suitable devotion.
For what myth can explain the blind earnestness
with which I hold out my best part to a lover whose gaze
is turned inward, whose feathers are damp
and already shifting beneath my hand.

🖋 Ornithology

What if heaven is this day, slightly humid,
or the indigo bunting outside my window,
distractedly pecking among the grasses for seed.
Like anyone, I have my superstitions, am subject
to a god of punishment and wrath, and I would like
to be visited by the Holy Ghost if it meant
I'd learn to love my suffering. But the world is good
and continually itself. Hungry, parched,
on a path that cuts through towns and villages
leaving carnage in its wake, it never thinks
of the observer. And that fingerprint of color
at the heart of those bushes
is not the bluebird of good fortune, no matter what
the field guide says and even the cardinal,
for all its brazenness, now seems commonplace.
All the same, it never fails to capture
my attention, and every afternoon I wait for indigo
to appear like a blue coal among the branches,
bringing me out of my chair to stand at the window
with my mouth open, holding my breath.

◖ The Swimmer

For the few weeks we lived together
he seemed foreign, unknowable, so I
have made him a son, picturing us
in a quiet apartment, gazing out windows
from the difficult life I have refused.
I've never thought in this way
about the first, who came
when I was young enough to fear the procedure
and not the palpable absence and regret,
nor of the next, conceived
without love or affection. But this last
lived in me differently: not like a disease
but as if he meant to persist, to continue
occupying my cells with water and blood.
I said good-bye
with my hands pressed to the place
where I imagined a bundle of cells
mercilessly dividing and turned my face
towards the anesthetist before I went under.
And afterwards, was I less empty
than before—wiped clean but for the dull ache,
the guilty relief? Still, he lingers, or I do,
trying to picture a face, fat and dark-eyed
like mine was but paler, but he won't stay
put in the world of children
who surpass the stage of gilled swimmer,
and are envisioned with their five
substantial fingers balled
into insistent human fists. All I have left
of his brief residence are cryptic
dreamed images. In one he had plastic limbs

and the fixed blue gaze
of my favorite doll and later
a furred animal head emerged
from between my thighs. It returned to me
mid-day as I stood beneath the shower, the bitter residue
of a rich meal that made
all the tastebuds lining my tongue
stand up and remember.

❦ Evolution

You are talking on the phone,
about your day or job, living
what you've grown to count on
like morning, the way you suppose
your voice will emerge, when suddenly
you announce something unexpected,
utter a word or hear the wrong response
cross the wire and flush your ear with pain,
and when you hang up the phone
even the street looks strange, shabbier
than you remembered
and the houses contain a world formed
while your back was turned, while you
were looking elsewhere.
Maybe you want someone you didn't know
you wanted. Maybe you are moving house.
Maybe this sourness and spastic stomach
are what the first amphibian tasted
the day its gills sprouted into lungs,
and unaccountably tired of swimming
or out of curiosity, it threw itself
onto a nearby, craggy shore
and when it opened up its mouth in surprise
at the rough dark earth beneath its breast
and the sudden stillness, it was already too late
to slide back into the primordial soup,
it was breathing. How different
the sun must have felt
from that position, bearing down,
relentless, altering the texture
of that first amphibian's brown
slimy skin. And lying there, with its stomach
in an uproar, maybe its water life, the grappling

after bottom dwellers, the endless
snuffling among cracked shells
and other detritus, all that swimming
and diving, began to seem like
just one of many possibilities
or even a kind of drowning.

❧ Release

I have been the woman on the subway
who cannot keep, whose forehead
bears the mark of bewilderment,
the one you turn from to grant relief
from the searing self-loathing self-spectacle.
And I have recognized her crying
on the treadmill and looked away
or looked too long, become entangled.
One year almost every night I woke unnaturally
to the sound blood makes
as it streams from heart to brain and thrums
inside the capillaries. I wore my weariness
and could not abide the coloring book's instructions:
reserve red for the arteries, blue for veins
and green for the bile ducts. Every vessel
colored green against the ones
whose loves remained, for the man
who woke satisfied with morning,
even for one who suffered
not the failure of love
but of the loved one's much loved body.
I agree that grief can make the world expand
and stretch your skin to a dazzling luster, but today
I was glad to be the one to turn away
or look on in silence, that the heaviness
that entered the room was an inexact fit
and my own was elsewhere,
biding its time, that during those moments
sorrow smoothed my tousled hair
but did not linger.

At the Heart of the Season

After a few false starts,
I tear into the brambles and stumble back
to the clearing and the low
stone wall where I can rest
before I worry down the wooded hillside
defeated. That's when I see it: blue-green hills
folding into the distance, a plumed cacophony of trees
at a horizon that's always been there
like these stones and fallen yellow weeds.
Long scratches swell to reddish welts
along my legs. They say look, the steepledowne
is pink and white, the barn swallows cry
against a sky that is empty and clean,
the black-edged butterflies whirl up in flight
and the sexual hum of crickets rubs into the air,
for with each day the world is washed new
beneath the covers of the night
and even the horsefly biting your shoulder
insists *love this, love this.*

❧ Entry

Let the sea in my window every morning
remind me of the world and its long
thirsty life. Let me ask. Let me admit.

Let me draw myself into the picture
where everyone stands close together conversing
and not focus on the space that separates

one body from the other, deeds from intentions,
what is said from what is meant. Let me see instead
the eagerness with which they listen,

despite weariness from having crossed
wide distances to stand just so on this day, and notice
their shyness, the difficulty each has

returning the other's gaze, but especially
the way their hands hang listless
at their sides, or jump nervously from hip to chin

or rest protectively across their chests
just below the vulnerable heart. Let me speak
and nod my head and occasionally touch

someone else's shoulder, ignoring the hissing
vigilant voice that cautions *no*. Make me brave enough
to see my life as one more version of the human,
and exhausted enough to begin.

Donor

Even on TV, it makes me woozy,
and when it happens to me
I keep my eyes squinched up and lie down

for the briefest test. I don't love my blood
too much, or think it's sacred. It can leak
indecisively between chambers or rush

to stain my chest and neck at awkward
moments. Like anyone, I greet each month's
blood arrival with indifference, unmoved

by the bright slick against the tissue or burgundy
coagulation at the water's rim. And this blood
could upset, for each numbered egg

stinks of my own death as it carries off
the fragile unpaired chromosomes. The Japanese
believe in blood types the way other cultures

follow birth signs and numerology. *A* types
make good providers but should never marry *AB,*
my students warned me. Such a combination

could be dangerous. My friend's blood
made her own baby sick. No one had prepared her
and for two days she watched bewildered,

as he grew yellow against her. How lonely
she must have felt when they washed
the poisoning cells from his body. My blood

would be acceptable to the heart
of nearly anyone. It could even bring you, my love,
back to health. I should give my blood away

in recognition of its willingness to run blue
through the arteries of a stranger and as security
against the day when its specificity could kill me,

for my blood is generous but must choose
its bedfellows carefully. Though I will always be afraid
when I feel it passing from my body, I want to give you

its healthy platelets, the hemoglobin
that carries oxygen and tints it red. I don't know
what type blood coils along your sinews

but I want mine to drench your heart and feed
your thoughts, fill your sex when it presses
into me, but mostly I offer you

its capacity to stop bleeding, to form a seal
over any scrape or cut, all the wounds
that have opened your skin.

for AMD

I would like to extend heartfelt thanks to Audrey Alenson, Frank Bidart, Jay Cantor, Stephanie Gaynor, Ellen Geist, Conrad Hilberry, Rick Poverney and Claudia Rankine for their invaluable support and advice; also to the other members of Alice James Books and Kinereth Gensler, Sharon Kraus and Adrienne Su in particular; and to Tony Dillof for these and many other forms of care.

Lisa Sewell was raised in California and studied Genetics and Marine Biology at the University of California at Berkeley, and creative writing at New York University. She has received grants and fellowships from the Massachusetts Cultural Council, the Fine Arts Work Center in Provincetown, the Bread Loaf Writers Conference and the Loft in Minneapolis. She teaches English and creative writing at Villanova University in Pennsylvania.

Recent Titles from Alice James Books

Suzanne Matson, *Durable Goods*
David Williams, *Traveling Mercies*
Margaret Lloyd, *This Particular Earthly Scene*
Timothy Liu, *Vox Angelica*
Alice Jones, *The Knot*
Jean Valentine, *The River at Wolf*
Rita Gabis, *The Wild Field*
Deborah DeNicola, *Where Divinity Begins*
Richard McCann, *Ghost Letters*
Doug Anderson, *The Moon Reflected Fire*
Carol Potter, *Upside Down in the Dark*
Forrest Hamer, *Call and Response*
E.J. Miller Laino, *Girl Hurt*
Theodore Deppe, *The Wanderer King*
Robert Cording, *Heavy Grace*
Cynthia Huntington, *We Have Gone to the Beach*
Nora Mitchell, *Proofreading the Histories*
Ellen Watson, *We Live in Bodies*
Kinereth Gensler, *Journey Fruit*
Adrienne Su, *Middle Kingdom*
Sharon Kraus, *Generation*

Alice James Books has been publishing poetry since 1973. One of the few presses in the country that is run collectively, the cooperative selects manuscripts for publication through competitions. New authors become active members of the press, participating in editorial and production activities. The press, which places an emphasis on publishing women poets, was named for Alice James, sister of William and Henry, whose gift for writing was ignored and whose fine journal did not appear in print until after her death.